Collins

English for Exams

Cambridge English

Movers

Three Practice Tests

for Cambridge English: Movers (YLE Movers)

Collins

HarperCollins Publishers
The News Building
1 London Bridge Street
London
SE1 9GF

First edition 2014

© HarperCollins Publishers 2014

ISBN 978-0-00-753597-2

Collins® is a registered trademark of HarperCollins Publishers Limited

www.collinselt.com

A catalogue record for this book is available from the British Library

Typeset in India by Q2A Media Services Pvt. Ltd

Printed and bound by Printing Express, Hong Kong

Author: Anna Osborn

Illustrators: Q2A Media Services Pvt. Ltd

Audio recordings: Dsound

Contents

Introduction

The Collins practice tests book for *Cambridge English: Movers* helps young learners to prepare for the *Cambridge English: Movers* test. These three practice tests reflect the structure and content of the official test, providing authentic practice for students at this level.

The Teacher's Guide and Parent's Guide are available for free online at www.collinselt.com. They contain a comprehensive overview of each section of the test so that teachers, parents and students can become acquainted with the test. They are also full of tips and ideas to help students to prepare for the test and they provide full answer keys, scripts for the Speaking papers and audio scripts of the recordings on the CD. They also include the official *Movers* vocabulary list.

The mp3 CD at the back of this book contains the recordings for the Listening papers as well as the scripts for the Speaking papers. These not only demonstrate the interchange that students can expect in the Speaking papers, but also give students the opportunity to practise speaking in English so that they can be fully prepared and confident about what to expect on the day of the test.

Blank page

Listening

Part I
– 5 questions –

Listen and draw lines. There is one example.

Alex   Bill   Nick   Daisy

Sally   Vicky   Tony

Part 2
– 5 questions –

Listen and write. There is one example.

Sports centre homework

	Comes:	every ....Saturday..........
1	Favourite sport:	....
2	Comes to sports centre by:	....
3	Comes to sports centre with:	his ....
4	Likes sports centre because:	it's ....
5	Name:	Mr ....

Part 3
– 5 questions –

What did Peter do last week?

**Listen and draw a line from the day to the correct picture.
There is one example.**

Monday

Tuesday

Wednesday

Thursday

Friday

Saturday

Sunday

Part 4
– 5 questions –

Listen and tick (✓) the box. There is one example.

What's the matter with Paul?

A ✓

B ☐

C ☐

1   Which man is Mary's father?

A ☐

B ☐

C ☐

2   What's Jane doing now?

A ☐

B ☐

C ☐

3   What did Fred have for breakfast today?

A ☐   **B** ☐   **C** ☐

4   What work does Sue's mum do?

A ☐   **B** ☐   **C** ☐

5   What present did Kim get yesterday?

A ☐   **B** ☐   **C** ☐

Part 5

– 5 questions –

Listen and colour and write. There is one example.

Blank page

Reading & Writing

Part 1
– 6 questions –

Look and read. Choose the correct words and write them on the lines. There is one example.

a whale

a clown

earache

a kitten

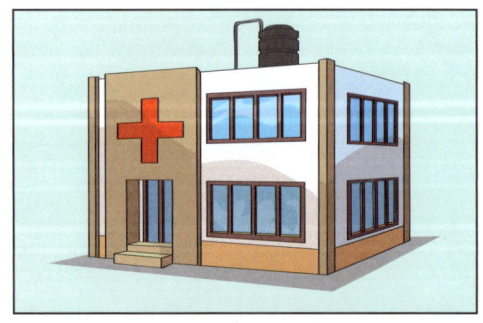

a hospital

a teacher

football

a doctor

Example

This person is very funny. ....a clown

Questions

1 You go and see this person when you are
   not well.   ....

2 This is a baby cat.   ....

3 You have this when your ears hurt.   ....

4 You go to this place when you are not well.   ....

5 You kick a ball with your feet to play this sport.   ....

6 This is the biggest animal in the world and
   it lives in the sea.   ....

Part 2
– 6 questions –

Look and read. Write yes or no.

Examples

There are four children in the park.   ....yes.............

There are four dogs in the park.   ....no.................

Questions

1   There are six ducks in the lake.   ....

2   Three girls are flying kites.   ....

3   The man with a grey moustache is reading
     a book.   ....

4   The boy who is wearing a green scarf is
     eating a burger.   ....

5   The girl with the long blonde hair is taller
     than the girl with the short brown hair.   ....

6   The boy who is wearing a sweater with a
     panda on it is giving some bread to the ducks.   ....

Part 3

– 6 questions –

Read the text and choose the best answer.

Paul is telling his friend Daisy about a film he saw at the cinema.

Example

| **Daisy:** | Hi Paul, did you enjoy the cinema? |

Paul:	A	Yes, I have.
	(B)	Yes, I did.
	C	Yes, I do.

Questions

1   **Daisy:**   Did you see the new film about lions in the jungle?

    Paul: A   Yes, I saw a film about pirates.

                  B   No, I saw a film about pirates.

                  C   Yes, I can.

2   **Daisy:**   What's the name of the film?

    Paul: A   It's called *Pirate Island.*

                  B   It's about pirates who find some treasure.

                  C   It was funny.

3 **Daisy:** Was the film exciting?

  Paul: A Yes, it was.

        B Yes, I did.

        C Yes, it can.

4 **Daisy:** Did you go with your friend Vicky?

  Paul: A No, she's eight years old now.

        B No, she couldn't come today.

        C Yes, she can play the guitar.

5 **Daisy:** Did you go by bus?

  Paul: A No, we went by train.

        B No, we went on Tuesday.

        C No, we can't.

6 **Daisy:** How often do you go to the cinema?

  Paul: A I go with my mother.

        B I go by bus.

        C I go every weekend.

Part 4
– 7 questions –

Read the story. Choose a word from the box. Write the correct word next to numbers 1–6. There is one example.

Last Tuesday, it was very sunny. Vicky went to the park with her mum.

They rode their .... *bikes* .... and took a picnic. When they got to

the park, Vicky played football with some children. Then Vicky and her

mum (**1**) .... their cheese sandwiches and drank some

(**2**) .... orange juice.

"I want to climb (**3**) .... now," said Vicky.

"What a good idea!" said Mum.

"I want to climb the (**4**) .... tree!", said Vicky.

"Be careful, Vicky," said Mum. "That tree is very tall."

Vicky climbed up the tallest tree, but she couldn't climb down again.

She (**5**) .... "Help me, please, Mum!"

Mum stood under the tree and Vicky jumped into her

(**6**) ....

"Thank you, Mum. I can climb up trees, but I can't climb down again!"

Example

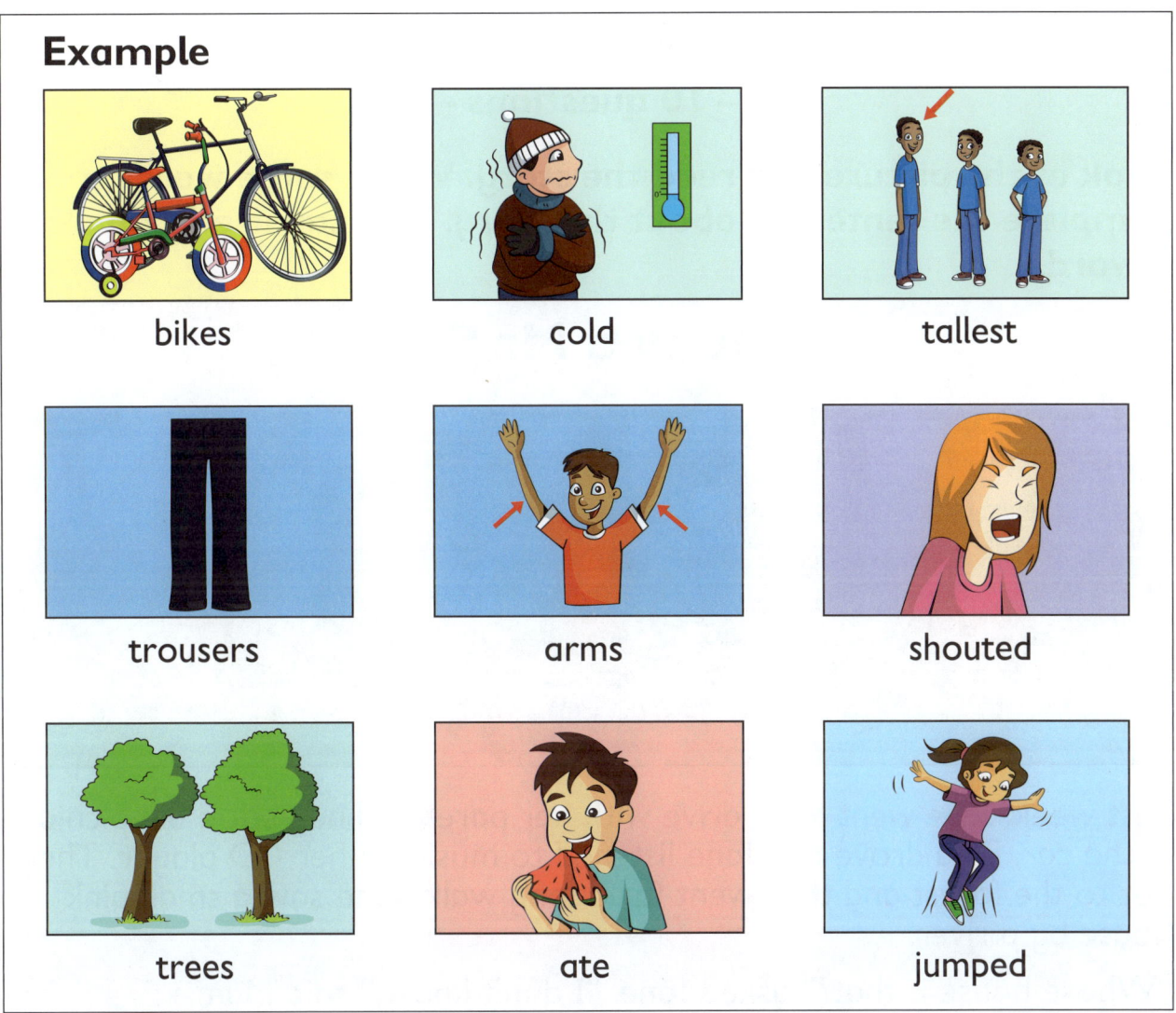

bikes

cold

tallest

trousers

arms

shouted

trees

ate

jumped

(7) **Now choose the best name for the story.**

Tick (✓) one box.

Vicky's exciting day at the park ☐

Vicky can't play football ☐

Vicky and Mum ride bikes ☐

Part 5
– 10 questions –

Look at the picture and read the story. Write some words to complete the sentences about the story. You can use 1, 2 or 3 words.

Jane and Mr Sam

Last week, Jane went for a drive with her parents. They put a big picnic in the car. Dad drove and Jane listened to music on her CD player. They got to the forest and they went for a long walk. Jane saw a small pink house by a river.

"Whose house is that?" asked Jane. "I don't know," said Mum.

They stopped and ate their picnic. Then they sat under a tree and Jane listened to Mum who told her a story.

"There was a little girl called Jane who went for a walk in a forest and saw a nice bear called Mr Sam…"

Jane was very tired. She closed her eyes and slept. She started to dream.

Examples

Jane and her parents went for a drive last ....*week*................ .

They took ....*a big picnic*............ with them.

Questions

1   There was a .... next to a river in the forest.

2   They sat under a tree and Mum told Jane ....

3   Jane slept and had a ....

"Hello, Jane," said a nice big brown bear, "my name is Mr Sam."

"I know," answered Jane. "My mum told me about you."

"Would you like to see my house?" asked Mr Sam.

"Yes, please," said Jane.

Mr Sam showed Jane his small pink house, which was next to a river.

"What a great house!" said Jane.

They went inside and had some cake and milk. Mr Sam gave Jane his old scarf to wear because she was cold. It was purple and white.

"You can take my old scarf home, Jane," said Mr Sam. "It's a present."

"Thank you," said Jane. "I love it."

4   Jane talked to a bear who was called ....

5   Mr Sam took Jane to see ...., which was next to a river.

6   Mr Sam's scarf was purple ....

7   Mr Sam told Jane that she could take .... home.

Then Jane woke up and said to her mother, "where did Mr Sam go?"

"Mr Sam isn't here, Jane. He's only in a story."

Jane told her mum that she went to Mr Sam's small house in the forest.

"It was a dream," said Mum. "Come on, let's go home."

Jane was sad because she liked Mr Sam. Then she saw the purple and white scarf, which was round her neck. She looked at the forest again and saw the nice big brown bear behind a tree.

"Goodbye, Mr Sam," Jane said very quietly. "Thank you again for the beautiful scarf."

Mr Sam smiled at her and waved goodbye.

8   When Jane ...., she asked for Mr Sam.

9   Jane's mum said that Mr Sam was only a bear
     ....

10   But Jane saw Mr Sam .... and said goodbye
     to him.

Blank page

Part 6

– 5 questions –

Read the text. Choose the correct words and write them on the lines.

Sandwiches

Example You make a sandwich with bread. You can put cheese,
fish, meat or salad ....in.......... sandwiches. Children

1 sometimes take sandwiches .... school with them.
People sometimes eat sandwiches when they have a picnic.

2 In 1762, John of Sandwich .... the first sandwich,

3 which had meat in it. He was hungry but he ....
want to stop playing a game with his friends. He wanted
to eat his dinner between bread. The word "sandwich"

4 comes from .... name.

Now, there are Sandwich Days in some countries

5 .... lots of people eat sandwiches all day.

Example	out of	off	in
1	to	on	under
2	eating	ate	eats
3	don't	doesn't	didn't
4	her	his	their
5	when	which	who

Speaking

PICTURE STORY

ODD-ONE-OUT

Listening

Part 1
– 5 questions –

Listen and draw lines. There is one example.

Anna   Mary   Ben   Kim

Paul   Peter   Sue

Part 2

– 5 questions –

Listen and write. There is one example.

Mrs Jack's weekend

	Mrs Jack went to:	the .... mountains ....
1	She went with:	her .... Peter
2	Her friend's house is:	next to .... Lake
3	She was there for:	.... nights
4	They went for:	long ....
5	She went by:	....

Part 3

– 5 questions –

What did Daisy do last week?

**Listen and draw a line from the day to the correct picture.
There is one example.**

| Monday |

| Tuesday |

| Wednesday |

| Thursday |

| Friday |

| Saturday |

| Sunday |

Part 4
– 5 questions –

Listen and tick (✓) the box. There is one example.

What pet does Sally want to get?

A ☐

B ☐

C ✓

1   Where's Alex now?

A ☐

B ☐

C ☐

2   Which is Pat's teacher?

A ☐

B ☐

C ☐

3   What's the weather like today?

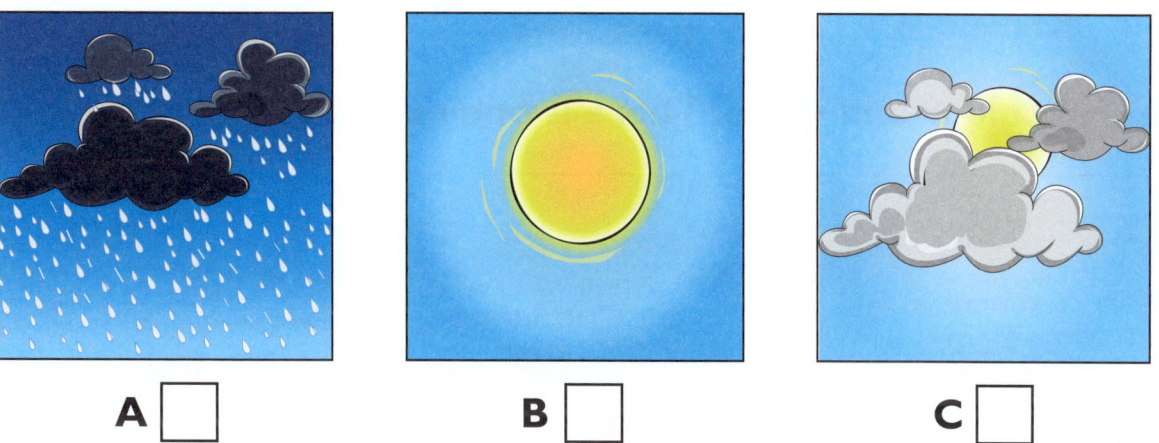

A ☐   B ☐   C ☐

4   What's the film that Jane is watching about?

A ☐   B ☐   C ☐

5   Where's Jill's homework?

A ☐   B ☐   C ☐

Part 5

– 5 questions –

Listen and colour and write. There is one example.

Blank page

Reading & Writing

Part 1
– 6 questions –

Look and read. Choose the correct words and write them on the lines. There is one example.

tea

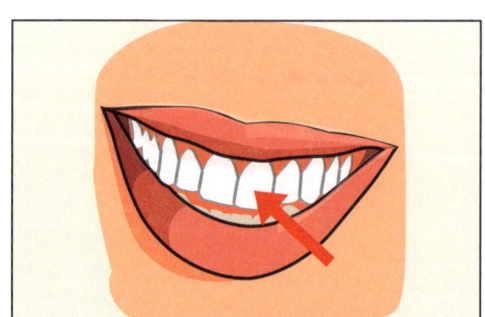

teeth

a picnic

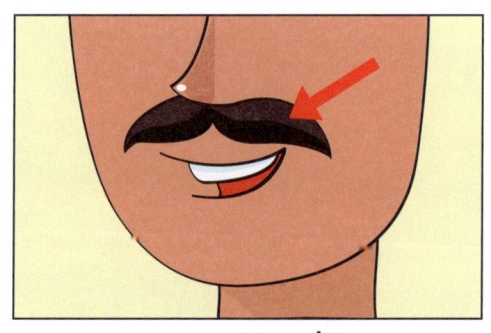

a moustache

juice

a library

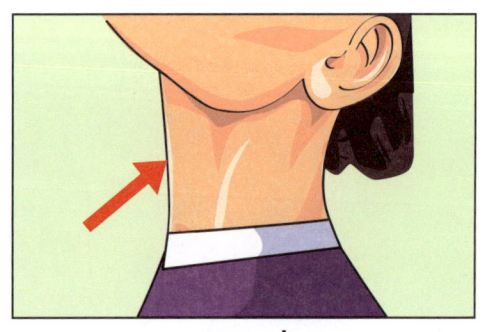

a neck

a supermarket

Example

This is hair that men sometimes have above their mouth.

.....a moustache.....

Questions

1   You can find lots of books in this place.

....

2   You use these white things inside your mouth when you eat food.

....

3   You can buy food and other things in this place.

....

4   This part of the body is between the head and the shoulders.

....

5   This hot drink is made with leaves which sometimes come in a bag.

....

6   This is food that you eat outside.

....

Part 2

– 7 questions –

Look and read. Write **yes** or **no**.

Examples

There are three cows in the field near the people. ....yes.............

There is a farmer in the field near the people. ....no.............

Questions

1   Two women and two children are
    having a picnic.   ....

2   The woman who is wearing purple
    glasses is laughing.   ....

3   The biggest bird is eating a sandwich.   ....

4   The girl who is pointing to the bird is
    younger than the girl with the red trousers.   ....

5   The woman who is wearing a yellow
    shirt is drinking some orange juice.   ....

6   There are apples on the tree behind the people. ....

Part 3
– 6 questions –

Read the text and choose the best answer.

Peter is talking to his mother about his first day at a new school.

Example

Mum:	How was your first day at school, Peter?
Peter:	A Yes, I can.
	B No, I don't.
	Ⓒ It was good.

Questions

1   **Mum:**   What's your new teacher called?

    Peter: A   She's got long brown hair.

                       B   She wore a green sweater.

                       C   Her name is Mrs Field.

2   **Mum:**   Do you like her?

    Peter: A   Yes, she's very nice.

                       B   Yes, she can walk.

                       C   Yes, please.

3   **Mum:**   Is she old?

    Peter: A   No, she's nice.
                       B   Yes, she's young.
                       C   No, she's young.

4   **Mum:**   Are there a lot of new children in your class?

    Peter: A   Yes, there is.
                       B   No, there isn't.
                       C   No, there aren't.

5   **Mum:**   Did you sit next to your friend Jim?

    Peter: A   No, I couldn't because he's in another class.
                       B   Yes, I have.
                       C   No, I'm not.

6   **Mum:**   Do you want something to eat?

    Peter: A   Yes, please. I'm thirsty!
                       B   Yes, please. I'm hungry!
                       C   No, I didn't.

Part 4

– 7 questions –

Read the story. Choose a word from the box. Write the correct word next to numbers 1–6. There is one example.

Last Saturday, Mary and Jim went for a drive in the ....*countryside*.......... with their Uncle Sam. It was a (**1**) .... day. They saw a beautiful forest and a big mountain. Then they came to a farm.

"Let's go and see the farm," said Uncle Sam. "I think it's open."

The farmer (**2**) .... at them when he saw them. "Would you like to see some animals?" he asked.

"Yes, please," said the children.

Mary gave some food to the chickens and Sam gave some water to the cows. Then they all went for a (**3**) .... on some brown horses.

"I like all the animals," said Mary. "But I like (**4**) .... best."

"Me too," said Jim.

Then they had to go home. They said goodbye to the farmer and (**5**) .... home. They were (**6**) .... but very happy.

Example

countryside

horses

tired

drove

smiled

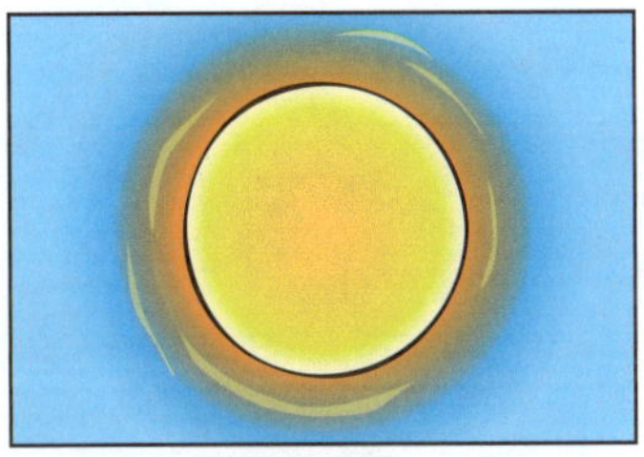

sunny

ride

spider

sang

(7) **Now choose the best name for the story.**

Tick (✓) one box.

The children go for a drive ☐

Chickens are the best ☐

A busy day at the farm ☐

Part 5
– 10 questions –

Look at the picture and read the story. Write some words to complete the sentences about the story. You can use 1, 2 or 3 words.

Let's find the treasure!

Last Tuesday was an exciting day for Fred and his family. A big lorry came to their old house and took all their things to a new house, which was in a village near the sea. Fred and his parents drove in their car with their dog Ben. When they got to their new house, Fred ran upstairs to his new bedroom.

Fred was very happy because his new bedroom was the best room in the house. It was on the top floor and he could see the sea from his window. He took all his things out of the boxes and put them in his new room.

Examples

Fred and his family had ....*an exciting day*.... last Tuesday.

Their new house is ....*in a village*.... near the sea.

Questions

1   Fred, his parents and their .... drove to their new house.

2   Fred's new bedroom was on .... of the house.

3   From his bedroom window, Fred .... the sea.

Then Fred was surprised to see something white on the wall of his bedroom. He took it down and looked at it carefully.

"What do you think it is, Ben?" Fred asked his dog.

Then Fred understood that it was a map of the garden. There was a big letter "X" on the map.

"It's a treasure map," said Fred. "I want to find the treasure! Come on, Ben, let's go and look in the garden."

4   Fred found a white thing .... of his bedroom.

5   It was .... the garden, which had an "X" on it.

6   Fred went to the garden to look for ....

In the garden, Fred looked at the "X" on the map and found the correct place under a big tree and next to a plant. But Fred couldn't see any treasure. Ben put his nose on the ground and looked under the plant. Then the clever dog found an old box and showed Fred.

"Well done, Ben, you found it!" Fred said.

On the box, Fred read the words, "A present for the new boy of the house from the old boy of the house". Fred opened the box very slowly and saw that there were lots of old comics and toys inside. What a great box of treasure!

7   Fred found the right place in the garden under a big tree and
     .... a plant.

8   Ben found an old box under ....

9   The box was a present from .... of the house.

10   Inside the box were many old ....

Blank page

Part 6
– 5 questions –

Read the text. Choose the correct words and write them on the lines.

Bears

Example

Bears are big, strong animals ....which........ eat both meat and plants. They are different colours and some are big

1 and .... are small.

2 They have hair .... their bodies.

3 Sometimes, they can be loud and angry. .... they are clever and are good at hiding too. They have four legs

4 but they can stand on .... two back legs when they have to. They can climb and run quickly.

5 Bears often .... in forests or mountains and some live in very cold places in the snow.

Example	where	which	when
1	some	any	all
2	in	under	on
3	Because	Than	But
4	my	their	his
5	live	lived	living

Speaking

FIND THE DIFFERENCES

PICTURE STORY

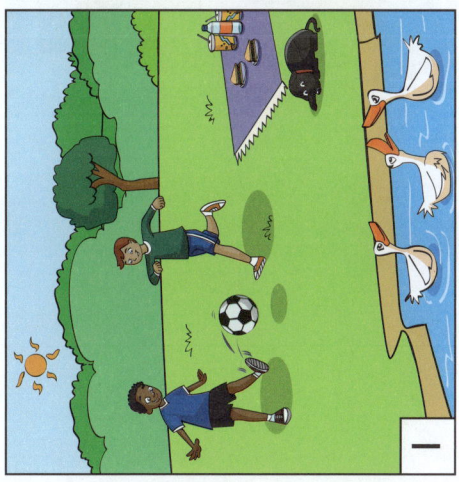

ODD-ONE-OUT

Listening

Part 1
– 5 questions –

Listen and draw lines. There is one example.

Bill   May   Tom   Lucy

Jim   Fred   Jane

Part 2
– 5 questions –

Listen and write. There is one example.

Mr Beard's new pet

	Mr Beard's pet is a:	.... *Kitten* ....
1	Colour:	....
2	Age:	.... *weeks*
3	Likes to:	*run and* ....
4	Eats?	*Kitten* ....
5	Name?	....

Part 3
– 5 questions –

What did Paul do last week?

**Listen and draw a line from the day to the correct picture.
There is one example.**

Monday

Tuesday

Wednesday

Thursday

Friday

Saturday

Sunday

Part 4
– 5 questions –

Listen and tick (✓) the box. There is one example.

What does Nick want to do today?

A ☐   B ✓   C ☐

1   What part of her body did Pat hurt?

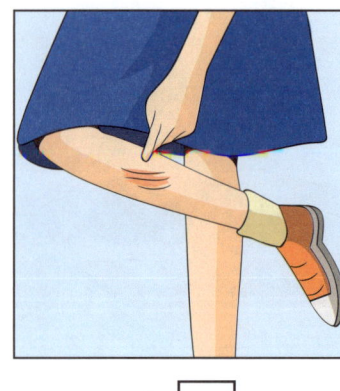 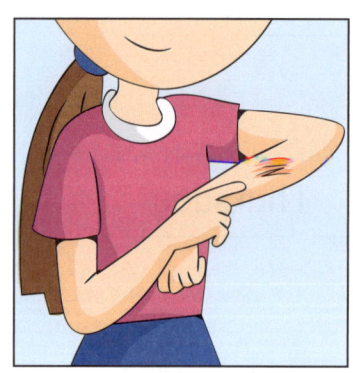 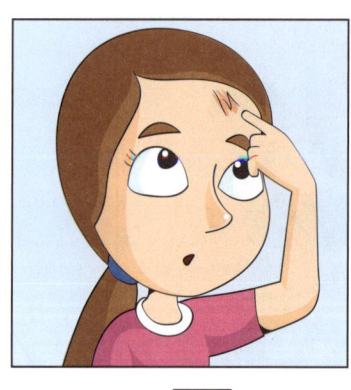

A ☐   B ☐   C ☐

2   What animal did Sally see at the farm?

A ☐   B ☐   C ☐

3   What does Peter want to do on his birthday?

A

B

C

4   What did Mary lose at the park?

A

B

C

5   What does Tom have to drink?

A

B

C

Part 5
– 5 questions –

Listen and colour and draw. There is one example.

Blank page

Reading & Writing

Part 1
– 6 questions –

Look and read. Choose the correct words and write them on the lines. There is one example.

a panda

a scarf

a puppy

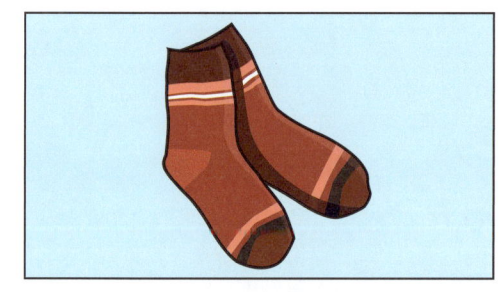

socks

a bedroom

a lion

a coat

a basement

Example

This is a big, strong animal that comes from the cat family. ....*a lion*...........

Questions

1   You wear this on your neck when it is cold. ....

2   This animal is a baby dog. ....

3   You go to this room in a house to sleep. ....

4   You wear these on your feet. ....

5   You go downstairs to get to this part of a house under the ground. ....

6   This big animal is black and white and can climb trees. ....

Part 2

– 7 questions –

Look and read. Write yes or no.

Examples

It is a cloudy day. ....*yes*...............

There are three buses at the bus station. ....*no*...............

Questions

1   The woman who is wearing a pink shirt is
    listening to her CD player.   ....

2   The woman with long brown hair is giving
    the baby a bottle of milk.   ....

3   There are three boys in front of the woman
    with the baby.   ....

4   The tallest boy is eating a banana.   ....

5   The boy who is wearing green trousers
    has got blonde hair.   ....

6   The youngest boy is holding a toy helicopter. ....

Part 3
– 6 questions –

Read the text and choose the best answer.

Fred is asking his friend Sally about her day.

Example

Fred:	Where did you go today, Sally?
Sally:	A I can play the piano.
	B I like ice cream.
	Ⓒ I went to Mary's party.

Questions

1   **Fred:**   Was it a good party?

    Sally: A   Yes, it was great.

                    B   Yes, I am.

                    C   Yes, it did.

2   **Fred:**   Were there lots of children there?

    Sally: A   No, there isn't.

                    B   No, there were only eight children.

                    C   Yes, it was sunny.

3   **Fred:**   What did you do?

    Sally: A   Yes, it was good.

                        B   No, I didn't.

                        C   We played games and climbed trees in
                             the garden.

4   **Fred:**   Did Mary like the present you gave her?

    Sally: A   Yes, I did.

                        B   Yes, she did.

                        C   Yes, she has.

5   **Fred:**   Did Mary have a nice cake?

    Sally: A   Yes, she had a lemon cake.

                        B   Yes, I have.

                        C   Yes, please.

6   **Fred:**   Was Mary's grandmother there?

    Sally: A   No, she couldn't.

                        B   Yes, she was.

                        C   She doesn't know.

Part 4
– 7 questions –

Read the story. Choose a word from the box. Write the correct word next to numbers 1–6. There is one example.

Yesterday it was sunny and very hot. John and Daisy went to the park and played football. Then John stopped the game and ...._sat_............ on the grass.

"What's the matter, John?" asked Daisy.

"I don't know," answered John. "But I have a (**1**) .... and I'm very thirsty."

Daisy took her friend to her house because Daisy's mother was a (**2**) ....

When Daisy's mum saw the children, she (**3**) .... them two big glasses of water. "Did you take your hats and some (**4**) .... of water with you to the park?" she asked.

"No, we didn't," said Daisy.

Daisy's mum said, "When it's very (**5**) .... you must (**6**) .... lots of water and you have to wear a hat."

"My head is better now," said John. "But I don't want to play in the sun again today."

Example

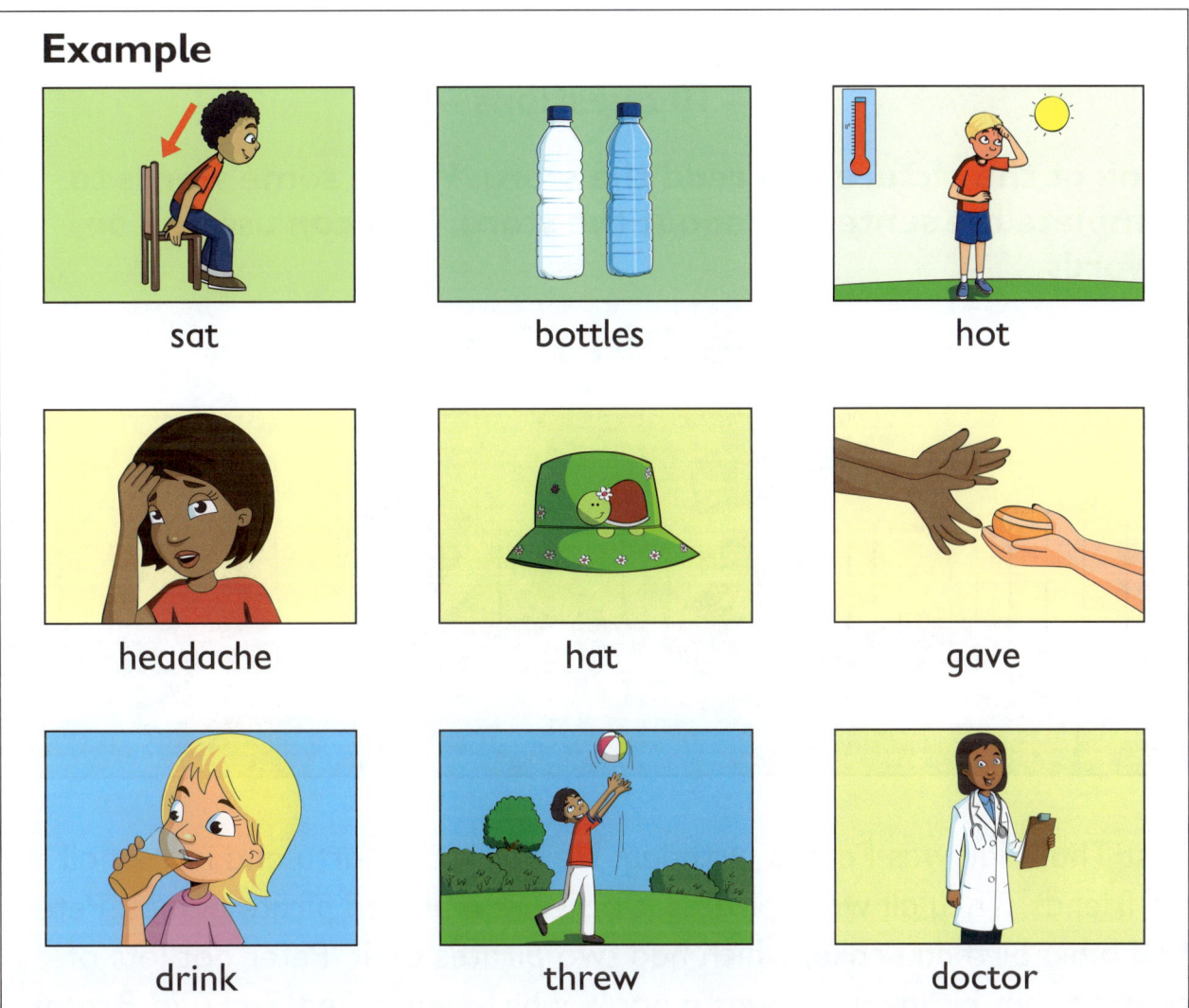

sat

bottles

hot

headache

hat

gave

drink

threw

doctor

(7) **Now choose the best name for the story.**

Tick (✓) one box.

Playing in hot weather ☐

John goes to the doctor ☐

Daisy plays football ☐

Part 5
– 10 questions –

Look at the picture and read the story. Write some words to complete the sentences about the story. You can use 1, 2 or 3 words.

The Old Pirates

Last Thursday was Peter's birthday. He had a big party and invited all his friends. They all wore pirates' clothes and played pirate games. Peter had a big birthday cake, which had two pirates on it. Peter got lots of presents but his favourite was a book, which was called *The Old Pirates.*

Examples

It was ......*Peter's birthday*...... last Thursday.

Peter invited ......*all his friends*...... to a big party.

Questions

1   All the children .... pirates' clothes and played pirate games.

2   There were .... on Peter's birthday cake.

3   Peter's favourite present was .... called *The Old Pirates.*

After his party, Peter sat in the garden and started to read his new book. It was an exciting story about two good pirates. Their names were Black Beard and Brown Beard. Black Beard was taller than Brown Beard and Brown Beard was stronger than Black Beard. They sailed the sea and found lots of treasure. But the pirates were old and they wanted to stop being pirates and live quietly in a nice house with a small garden with beautiful flowers.

"What a great book!" said Peter. "I'm enjoying it. I want Black Beard and Brown Beard to find a nice place to live."

4   Peter read his new book in ....

5   Black Beard was .... than Brown Beard.

6   The pirates wanted to .... in a nice house.

7   Peter thought that the new book was ....

Then a loud lorry stopped outside the house opposite. Peter looked at the lorry and saw two men. They carried big boxes into the house. Both men had beards. The man with the black beard was taller than the man with the brown beard. The man with the brown beard was stronger than the man with the black beard. The two men smiled and waved at Peter. Then they walked into their nice house, which had a small garden with beautiful flowers.

"I think the pirates from my book found their new house," said Peter.

8   Peter saw .... with beards outside the house opposite.

9   The man with the brown beard was .... than the man with the black beard.

10   Peter thought that the two men were .... from his book.

Blank page

Part 6

– 5 questions –

Read the text. Choose the correct words and write them on the lines.

Fishing

Example | Fishing is something that lots of different people ....*do*........ .
Many people enjoy fishing as a hobby – sometimes they

1 | .... the fish home to eat and sometimes they

2 | put them back .... the water. Some people
go fishing as their work and some people go fishing as a

3 | sport to see who can get the .... fish.

4 | Fish are good to eat. But we must .... careful not to

5 | take too .... fish from the sea because in some parts
of the world there are not a lot of fish now.

Example	do	don't	does
1	took	take	taking
2	in	on	behind
3	big	bigger	biggest
4	are	be	being
5	any	many	every

Speaking

FIND THE DIFFERENCES

PICTURE STORY

ODD-ONE-OUT